Growing up in Westchester
REVISITED

CHARLES T. JAMES

Copyright © 2020 by Charles James.

ISBN-9781645506997

All rights reserved. No part of this book may be reproduced or transmitted in any form or by any means, electronic or mechanical, including photocopying, recording, or by any information storage and retrieval system, without permission in writing from the copyright owner.

The views expressed in this work are solely those of the author and do not necessarily reflect the views of the publisher, and the publisher hereby disclaims any responsibility for them.

Matchstick Literary
1-888-306-8885
orders@matchliterary.com

INTRODUCTION

Growing Up In Westchester revisited. Let's visit it's early history. This is a town with roots dating back to the Revolutionary War. Turk's Head a public house as it was called back when Pennsylvania was growing. Its location was at the intersection of Wilmington to Reading Road with a section " Jefferies Ford to Philadelphia. Today these roads are Gay and High Streets. Still the same names of the streets that held a skirmish against the British. That battle; the Battle of Brandywine took place in Westchester against the British. Two British Soldiers were killed Later Goshen Township would set aside (1120) acres of land. They'd changed the name to Westchester. Westchester executed a black female, named, Hannah Miller. Year 1805! Strange that I'd put her name in this manuscript; my mother's stepfather was a Miller. I'd wonder if she'd "was any acquaintance to him? "Right! "I'm no writer. "Don't expect to get a Pulitzer Prize any time soon. "Furthermore; Let's get on with the story.

CHAPTER 1

"Growing up in Westchester! Let's see if we can keep you amused. The first book was an Author's Nightmare. Wrong editors! I'm not even an average writer. "Yeah it showed too"! I'm not a gambler, though, I'd took a beginner's role to writing a story about the town I'd grown up in. "Like in a game of Black Jack, I'd crapped out. My story begins. "Welcome if you will to 413 West Market Street. This is where the James Family resides. "Eventually this house would have ten family members too boast. Mom, dad included. "Ten too many! "Perfect reasoning not to have a large family; one that you can't take care of, at least more than you can manage to keep you from struggling to keep food on the table, and in their mouth, decent clothing on their body, etc. "It was hard to show your true emotions around the neighborhood, that your living in. "When the people that talk to you, were really talking about you, and smile, grin, even laugh in your face. "Now tell me, how much pride can you talk good things about your neighborhood, when all the odds are stacked against your family? "When your so called peers are putting you down, because of the clothes on your back as well as the shoes on your feet? "Just some of the many things that happened, to me as a little guy, now grown up, and has his own voice. "This is my last say. "Moving on, we'll talk about the house. It's a two bedroom house. "Borderline condemned property. "This house was Giving only to house a family that would never receive Section(8). "Dad, I'd have to say that, you'd didn't have the backbone too go out and make it possible to get a better home for your family. "Like I told you both that, I'm going to move to Pittsburgh too go back to school. "That took balls! "Too make a decision to leave home, against your parent wishes. "I'd might say this, that if you'd had done that dad, and said, honey! "I'll send for you, and the girls, "Once I'm established out here, in California. "No he'd settle for craps, he'd crap out. "We're now going to live in a slump home. "Rundown! It would need numerous work. "Indeed it would. There was only one small problem? Where do we get the money? "Dad don't have no money! "Habit-Tat-For Humanity didn't even exist. "Yet, mom thought that her aunt was hooking her up. "Guess not! "I sound ungrateful. "Yes I was! Due to the shame, torment, physical, mental abuse giving too me, my family brothers, by them many ignorant teens, and grownups in this town. "Hippocrates! "The world is full of them. "Yes I was pissed off! "Life has showed me that it's better to be pissed off, then pissed on. "But there's no worry. "Mom's auntie wasn't going to make us homeless. Regardless of code violations at 413 West Market Street. "They'd put in for housing. The Housing Authority was run by a man, who was a sex addict that only helped families get fast housing, only if the woman had sex with him. "Low income women have low standards. "Some don't care, just the results that follow. "Getting in to a new home was always the issue. "Most of the mothers of the families I'd known were loosey-goosey. "That jerk had made advances on my mom. "Knowing my mom she'd, put that fool in his place. "That's why we wasn't one of the fortunate families to get Section(8). "We'd stay right on 413 West Market Street until the end of my sixth year. "Mom, and dad just couldn't control their hormones. Every time there'd be another one added. "Enough that would make my life more miserable. Add to the clan it meant another mouth too feed. "This old house, it sounds like that television show, with one exception, they weren't fixing up this old house no time soon. We'd have to make do with what we'd have. "Let me start with dad. "Didn't have a father figure in his home. Raised by his mother, and her sister. Dad had an older brother. "Strange! "Dad never did talk much about his family. Would've been nice to know our family culture. Where our roots history begins. "A question could be asked, how are you an so an so related? And you'll ask yourself, I'd don't know the answer to that question, because no member in the family made it a priority to know who was in their family tree. I'd never met dad's mother. Dad's Aunt Grace was the aunt we'd children would learn to love enjoy every visit to her home. Above all else, She was an Amazing Grace, just like the song sings. "Her attention to detail was not to be challenged. "Shear respect. "We'd never leave her house with an empty belly. Excellent cook. Dessert were the bomb diggity. A word I'd made up for being dam good. Amazing Grace! That's what she was. Miss you! GOD BLESS! Dad could've been an entrepreneur. A talented man! Just poor! Back in the sixties there was this television show, "call The Ted Mack Amateur Hour". He'd audition as a singer. He'd got the attention of one of the manager's in a group; that was looking for a backup singer to sing with his Jazz Trio; featuring Jimmy Smith on keyboard, with a drummer, and add a guitar player. One catch; that was dad had to pay for his own transportation out to California. "Hollywood"! Believe it or not, dad made his impossibility a true reality. "He'd saved up just enough to make the audition. "There'd be extra money for travel expenses. Not only did he win! "Certainty lingered in the mix. "Can you believe it! "My dad's in the big time! "Backup singer! "Who would've thought that! It's funny how murphy's law come's into the picture. "Whatever is meant to go wrong, it will. Here now, Dad's all the way out in Hollywood, California, gets a phone call from his mom; stating that he's about to become a father. Dad's mom was always able to get in touch with him, just in case of an emergency. "Now stop the presses! ".He's about to live his dream. "What parent wouldn't want their child to live their dream, Now that it's happening? "She'd should've been proud. "Instead! "His readymade family would cause him too struggle ."Mom, I'd would've said, I'll send for them. "MY BIG BREAK! "Send some money when you can. "No! Dad decided to throw his dream away. Then he'd have to make it back to the east coast, the best way he could. The group would take a collection for dad. It'd only get him as far as the state of Illinois. Dad would take it to the road.

CHAPTER 2

Too the road. Dad would hitchhike from Illinois to Pennsylvania east coast bound! That wouldn't be as easy a journey than he'd thought it would be. Illinois is a state that I'd wouldn't get caught dead in. Figure of speech. "No for real! "Filled with angry people! "That's how I'd remember it when I was working in the city of Chicago, and the city of Joliet, Illinois. "That's when I'm working as a security worker for a private firm. "That's a state of angry people indeed! "Okay !" It's a nice place to visit in the summertime. It's extremely freezing cold weather. "When old man winter decides to sneeze, be indoors. Unless you're a Polar Bear. "Then that's your place too ramble. " Par from working in Illinois, it does have a few unique visiting places that I'd recommend you'd checkout. "Chicago is off the charts. " Despite all they're special spots to hangout, but still, no way can you get me to live there. You'd couldn't even pay me a large dowry to live there. "Too cold! Most people that do live in that state, usually, if athletic, I'll see them playing for a warm climate state. "For this reason, dad! " I'm asking; why not stay where you were? "That's a fare question! "I think I know the answer! "Fear! "Afraid of making it big. "That's what you'd did pop. "If you'd had had a coach to help you through your most trying emotions. Maybe you'd have made a better choice. "Things would've gotten better. Perhaps! "But you'd chose to be a coward. "Out in the Midwest; after making it that far; what was going through your mind? "Sure you'd known cold weather, but Illinois is a different kind of cold. "Hitch-hiking was probably no big deal when you were on the road then. But you were up there close to Lake Michigan. "Did it ever occur to you how close you were too Lake Michigan? " Gets cold at night. "Yeah pop's on the road. Left what could've been his moment in the spotlight. " Must've had some fear! " I've witnessed, some big want to be tuff guys buckle under from the mighty swells that the ocean would unleased while at sea. "Dad's family was praying hard for him to get home safe. Most likely his mom, and auntie was doing all the praying. Two church going ladies. "But it would've been much better for him to stay right where he was at. "Stay dad, if only some little bird got in his ear and pointed out to him, what he would be throwing away from California, by going back home. "That was your moment of truth. "How could you put forth all that effort to be on The Ted Mack Amateur Hour. "Than just give it all back? "If you're the go to guy, than step up and be the man. "Woman are more happy when they know you have a fat bank account. "Not an empty wallet! "Dad you should've stayed. "Make them share in that vision, you'd created. "He'd have a tall tale to tell, too the folks back home that doubted his intention. "I'd been living out there in sunny California. "Growing up there, I'd would've known celebrities! "Who knows could of been one myself. "His destiny was for seen by the All Mighty. Not a good gambler, "henceforth he'd be walking on a long highway road, waiting for somebody nice enough to stop an offer him a ride. "Dark, dark, roads! "Many more many dark roads to follow. "Hmm, pop! "Did you see or hear any wild animals? "The Bible say's; God protects fools, and babies. "Consequently, he'd said his singing would keep his mind off the cold when it was time to start walking again. "I'd couldn't have done it. "Couldn't even calculate how much walking was done in between rides. "Just kept on walking until a vehicle felt sorry for him. "Then offered him a ride. "That's how he'd hitchhiked from Illinois back to Westchester, Pennsylvania. "In good health, he'd made it back, but broke. "Too start his nightmare! "Not on Elm Street! "Still a nightmare. "Stop mopping! "Don't cry the blues! "Dad chose to be with mom, the two girls. "A love story! "What's that? They're only in movies. "Fantasies acted out on stage. "No mom! "No pop! "eight grade, eleventh grade total education level. "The game was over before it began. "Dad would become a drunk! "He'd argued all the time with mom. "It would get so bad that there'd be fighting on display for the whole block too witness. "While living on that block, it'd became story of events at school, the next day. "Now tell me how I'm I suppose too walk with my head held high, while the whole school children, it seemed to me, were making snickering remarks at me, some too my face, while others were laughing and grinning behind my back. "It was God's will that they'd didn't kill one another. "They'd be rumbling like two heavyweight fighters exchanging blows. "While the fighting was so bad, that's why I know today that it was the will of God. "Why they'd didn't kill one another, and have us children sent to a foster home. "What's love going do with it? "If what my parents had is called love I'll never understand it. A victim of two failed marriages of my own. That's how my resume reads! "Some say the third one is the charm. "Nope! "Three strikes, you're out!, "Who said Love is just like a baseball game? "Three strikes you're out! "That much, I agree. "Take your own chance, I did! "And too this, I'm truly happy being single." Both parents tried to give me sound advice, most of the time, I'd listen to them like a child is suppose too listen to a grownup, only I'd found out through experiences of my own trials, and tribulations that it paid to pay attention to detail. "Like they'd all the time say this; "never travel any place with no money. However, dad you'd just hitchhiked from the Midwest to the east coast. "No job, no bank role. "All this to comeback to raise a family of three. "There's no logic in what you'd done. "Work! " Have to get a job at once. The morale of dad's story was: a simple lesson in economics. "Don't turn your back, on opportunity, when it comes a knocking. "Still GOD decides how many blessing will come in your life. "But he'd didn't let God's spirit help him. "That's why he'd lost. Your mom, auntie taught you about GOD, why not call on him to help you with a very hard decision, that had to be made. "Instead of asking the Almighty for help, you'd let your pride and Satan defeat you. "Dad had the right teaching concept in mind, when he said, don't be like me be better! "These things had mattered too me after surveying his loses. "Determined not to make his mistakes. "Pay it forward! "Don't quit! "A quitter never quits! "A loser keeps on trying until he gets the prize. Dad did pass that on. "I'd wouldn't accept defeat in the speedball tournament. "Now he'd chose to fail than to embrace success. "Pop you'd couldn't see your reasoning for wanting to achieve success. Why'd you'd quit school? "What made you think that succeeding was going to be just handed too you on a silver platter? "You'd failed mom when you'd impregnated her. "Being in Hollywood was your million to one shot. "That's why you've should've stayed where you were. " It wasn't just for you anymore, it's for your family, that you'd excepted. "Don't be a drunk like me son, be better. "Try hard work! "But I know that it doesn't pay to work hard, than to come up short. The move to go into military would teach me the importance of work hard. "Never look over an easier way to get the job done. "Weigh all your facts! "Getting the right results is the name of the game. "Homecoming should be a time to celebrate. "Shouldn't it? "But dad's return is tasked with immediate work. "Like The Isley Brothers said in one of their songs ."He had work to do. "And how fast it was needed. "Dad was no stranger to hard work. "How much work could he handle? "Folly dominated lots of his choices. Why instead of pleasing family first, he'd found salvation in pleasing his no good drinking buddies. "Marriage is supposed to be equal partnership. "But that's what will happen without sound advice from them that been there done that. "Waiting for the breadwinner to returns home. "Can you feed the children? "You're the man of the house. "Total mouths to feed is five. This is counting him and mom too." Five that's just too many mouths without a skill set of some kind. "No trade, no high school diploma either!" Let's look at dad's situation: raised in a fatherless home; about to take on a readymade family, and at the present time no job. "Wouldn't want to walk in an unemployment office minus no credentials. "With mom expecting his child, that tells his story. "Needs to get to work fast. Mom's aunt is going to give her this rundown piece of a house, to help them get started. "We'd probably been better off staying in a large tee-pee with our own heating accommodations. That way all we'd have to do is take from our environment. "Dad and auntie wasn't seeing eye to eye on personal matters. "That's a no brainer! "A young man that my dad was, with no high school diploma, no skill set, and now tries to take on the impossible. "Impossible would be too raise a readymade family that included my mother. "I'm resting my thoughts on one hot night. "Now dad comes back home to deal with a woman, showing first off, he'd have nothing to bring to the table. "Quite an impression too confront a woman, my aunt, who at best was a millionaire, from the funeral business. "Dad at that time, you'd could've easily impressed her by following your dream. "Too become that singer! "Show mom's aunt, that you wasn't coming home empty handed. "A business venture, she'd invested herself by completing college. "That didn't seem too impossible her to a dream come true. "Problem that lots of young men have is that their always thinking with the wrong head.

"She'd risked all her time in school, and it paid off. "Achieved her college degree. Met a man, and together they'd opened up very successful funeral business. "Both combined their knowledge of the business, and it did take off. "A success story! " as her "So how you going to impress mom's aunt? "Dad couldn't deliver! "They'd just tolerated each other for the sake of my mother. "Uncle was too much of a business man to let himself, get caught up in less important matters of the family. "Truly a wise man that reflexed in his business success. "The house! "It'd would need a great deal of work. In need of a Home Improvement package. "But where? "There wasn't any home improvement programs on the market. "None that I'd they'd knew about. The needs for a decent home was noticeable from on lookers passing by the house. "Getting a renovation was something that wasn't going to happen to my family. "Cancel that order. "Rejected are the bid for our family, it's not approved. Like the "StarKist Tuna" commercial, sorry Charlie! At times I may sound bitter, this my chance to get it off my chest. " Dad comes back to raise a family. "As a child I'm too embarrassed to walk down the street with my head held high, because I'm always wearing hand me down clothes. "I'd have no pride! "Just humiliation! "There were times when I'd wished that I'd wasn't born. "In first grade, I'd have a reversible suit which I'd change over every other day. "Wearing that suit, at first made me fill real cool. "Then after time would pass, I'm still wearing the same darn clothes. "After all this time, I'm starting to realize that my family is poor. "My family would struggle thanks to incompetents. "Add this to the quandary, they'd didn't know how to stop making children. Nor provide us with an adequate housing facility. "mom and dad "We were just another needy family in need of housing. "Section Eight we'd never get. "Barely received welfare. "The system sucked! "It would tell me that I was glad to have not been a recipient of welfare. "The people that ran the welfare programs were a bunch of snobs that thought their shit didn't stink. "Consequently because my mother's aunt had a successful funeral business, our family was denied assistance from the welfare people. "Excuse was always given that dad made too much money. "That was a big laugh. "We were poor as dirt and the house that we'd lived in was all the proof needed for the welfare program to assist us. "Mom's aunt was hated by people, the same two face clowns, that smiled in mom's face. "Making her think that they actually cared about her. "She just couldn't see what I saw as a child. "How phony, fake, some timey people, that they were. Who'd turned their noses up at the children, me one of them, while all the time grinning in mom's face, if she was present in their company. "Another reason I'd s stay mad for being her child. "She'd blown it! "So did dad! "And the children would pay the price for their lack of family education. "The neighborhood where I'd lived were a bunch of drunks, people that were down on their luck. "The losers dwelled there! "This one gentleman, him and his women lived in their car. "That was sad! "No place too cleanup. "Remembering this statement from mom, and dad too never make fun of people who have fallen on hard times. "I'd thank God too this day that I'd listen to them. "My parents made their share of mistakes. I'd used to fill like this; when they'd give out advice, I'd think like this: "How can you look forward to something, when those that are in charge are setting poor examples by their own selfish demeanor. "Luck would save me from a fate of shame. "This I can say now that I'm grownup. "Wasn't no available charity for the James Family. "Thank God I'm grown. "I'd hated back as a child when they'd show on the news how a family was chosen to get a new home. Well our family wasn't never placed in the drawing. "Not at all! "Never picked for anything but hard times. "Yes I blame the parents, because man should think with the right head and not the other. "Especially when they start thinking about raising children that you keep making minus an income. I thank the Lord Above for not letting me make the same mistakes that my dad made. "Yes I'm not ashamed to speak about my past. "I'd weathered the storm, through many, many a frustrated nights. "This is my story; an old song that needed to be told. "This old house. "I'd liked that program. "But it wasn't to be for the James. "I'm speaking about getting a decent home to live in. "The house for starters: the side door was always exposed to draft. That was the area that received the most traffic. In that foyer area, once inside the house, a shower was place against the wall near the bathroom. "Privacy was out of the question! "If one was in the shower, it would be better, you'd dressed inside the shower. "In and out, there the traffic kept flowing, most of the time it was us children. "I say again it didn't offer no privacy. "Someone comes in the door, if you're in the shower, hope that there heading for the living room or down to the cellar. "The draft, from the cold would be there to greet you. "Plus, there were perverts lurking in the neighborhood. "Dad didn't understand that the people he'd invite to drink with were looking at mom, my three sisters with lustful eyes. "He couldn't connect the dots, that they'd be waiting for the chance to crack on my sisters or opportunity to stab him in the back. "Mom would tell me later how his so called best friend had made a pass at her. "This person had a family of his own. "But was looking for opportunity. "But I'm still talking about this old house. "Listing are areas that everybody checks out when there visiting. "How could you allow anybody to use your bathroom when the toilet floor needs fixing up? Ashamed was my answer for that question. "Next there wasn't adequate bathroom space .Cramped it was! But it had a built-in closet directly across from the toilet. "Little storage, then again, storage necessary to place wash clothes, and towels. There'd also be a window as if needed any more draft. Let's talk about the indoor foyer space or an extension shed; which all the time would be cluttered up with debris, such as: clothes, toys, newspapers, boxes etc. All the items we'd gathered did help us to fight back the draft. During the winter months it would get really cold. Plus you'd not want to spend too much time in the shower, at all. "A family sibling was always getting sick. Other than the foyer area; the basement was cold. It's the coldest part of the house. "That foyer/shed. " No wonder it was too cold" with a capital(C) Cold"! Why bother to go and freeze your buttocks off ,once you'd exit the shower. "Wintertime a quick shower was recommended. "Or fill up a basin with water that was heated up on the stove. "Out into the foyer/shed area, enter into the kitchen. If you'd like living outside with a dirt floor. "Yes I'm describing the kitchen floor. "It needed to be dug up, leveled, smoothed out, then cemented to make it look like a normal kitchen floor. "Finally add in some tile. "Add new everything else in the kitchen; stove, sink, refrigerator, cabinets, etc. You know the items that make a woman happy too want to spend time in her kitchen. "Where was Home Improvement when the James Family needed it. "Oh! "I know! "It wasn't even thought of yet. "Oops! "Dreaming too far into the future. Two windows along the back wall enabled you to see down to the alley. "Look around as far as a nosey person's eyes would focus on. Be careful! "You'd have to step up, when entering into the next room. "Stop! "Immediately to your right are the steps to take you upstairs. "Hold off the upstairs for now. "A door just after the steps leading down to our cellar or basement. "Cold in the wintertime! "Very cool in the summertime. "For insulation, we'd gather together all sorts of things, that insulated, would insure a warmer basement. "Find it, we can use it, just toss it in the cellar for the needed warmth. "Absorbing as much of the cold as possible, you know, that's how us poor people would do it. "You'll love being down there, in our basement come summertime, for it was a natural air conditioning unit. "Sure an ideal spot in the springtime too. "Still it's quite chilly down there. "Just have your jacket on hand. "Please remember this that, during the wintertime that you always keep that door closed after entering, or as you exist. "It almost felt like standing on the inside of a freezer. "It wasn't a very insulated cellar at all, so keep your heavy coat handy! "Go down into that cold basement if you dare. " Every year, we'd accumulate enough junk down there to start a Rumage sell. "There'd be this old timer that frequented the neighborhoods, from time to time; only during the summer months, and early fall. He'd collect your junk items, maybe give you some money. Probably if he'd saw a profit to make that's if you'd didn't notice the value of the item, he'd be haggling with you, he'd known exactly how to get you to sell it to him. "That was his job, rip you off. "The dining room was the next small portion of our house. "A two shelf cabinet inserted with just enough room too stuff more junk. "I'd say maybe six feet tall was the height of the cabinets. "Once we'd stuffed every available crevice space with leftover items, you'd start feeling a difference in the room temperature. "Needing a place to put spare whatever, we'd never have a problem. "Fill all vacant areas! "At most the overloading of empty spaces in our home was almost like an artist designing a portrait. "Our family knew how to bring the heat. "And did keep it going all night, and into the next day. "With the Coal Stove operating in full swing, all we'd needed to do was keep the house warm. "Don't let the fire go out from the stove. "It was families responsibility to keep it going. "You'd knew when it would get cold. "That meant; one we'd used up all our supplies of coal, which means, now one of the siblings would be taking a walk to the coal yard. "Most likely, I'd be one of the sibling's. "That's the only time nobody complained. "Got a keep it warm! "Bring the heat! "Keeping warm, we'd learn how to keep a cozy home by stuffing rags, like applying a pipe patch on a ship. "You'd didn't want to be ever apart of a ship that was hit by a torpedo. "Even if you were worn down from work already, just plain tired from home chores, you'd still wanted a warm home. "Insulation, insulation, keep the house warm! That's the key, "don't let any house member in the house get sick. "Doctor bills, parents can't afford to pay them. "By now I'd knew that dad wasn't a good family provider, just my dad! "I'd estimated the height of them cabinets, the highest one was maybe six feet tall, on the bottom level of the cabinets were, two closing doors with hooking attachments; used for closing the cabinet doors. Another cluttered spaced; that we'd crammed with excess whatever we'd have available to shove in there. First shelf; cluttered to the tee. Last shelf. Need I say more. Cluttered! You'd add a couch in that dining space, surround it with chairs, that's our dining room. "Mind you'd have to jockey your chair in position to watch television. "Wait a minute? "The stove! "Along with a Christmas Stocking shelf was straight along the wall behind the Coal Stove. "Lookup! "There'd be a hole in the ceiling. It would allowed the heat to rise from the stove to the rooms upstairs. We'd have a Coal Stove first. "Each year my eldest sisters along with myself, and another brother, would trek ourselves over to the east end of town to Hagertys Coal yard. "The boys never had a pair of gloves to wear, so mom would've us put on an extra pairs of socks. "Didn't help much. "Because when we'd got home our hands were frozen. "Mom would've us put them in running cold water. "After soaking them for a few minutes, the blood started to circulate once more. About or maybe it was the fourth grade, that we'd put the Coal Stove too rest. "Good riddance! "Not going to miss you fellow.

CHAPTER 3

"The summer would come, and with it a ruptured sewage line. "It sounded like an explosion. "Loud. "Sounding like somebody detonated dynamite. "Aftermath! "There's no explosion, just a large cleanup crew would be assembled in our bathroom. "That ruptured pipe in the bathroom required every member of the household. "The pipe that sounded like an explosion was the sewage line. "Mom notified her aunt. "She'd have a sewage tech or somebody qualified in plumbing. "Auntie would've the Sewage Tech People replace the pipe. "And that's all they'd did! "In the meantime our family would stay with another relative until the problem was fixed. "By then, the family would return back to the shack! " Ha ha ! "I mean the pipe was replaced. "However! "Excuse my sarcasm! " Right now I'm being facetious! "It smelled really bad! "Shit is what we'd have to cleanup. "Why? Because it's our home and you didn't want to catch an infection of any sort from all that harmful waste. "Read on! "Now the family had to remove all the excrement from the bathroom. "Sucks! "That's what the all hands on deck was assembled for. "Funny I'd said that, because I'd participated in my share of all hands on deck, as a US Navy Sailor. Into the bathroom, hauling that waste from the bathroom tub, the walls, including the floor. "All that shit went into the backyard. "Place the feces in the yard! Dad would yell out, like orders being given by a Drill Instructor. "That's what dad's command sounded like, being blurted out at us children. "As we'd did exactly as we were told. "It'll make excellent fertilizer, "dad kept on speaking.

"And so that's what we did. "At harvest time we'd had plenty of edible vegetables. Plus the whole block would've some free veggies from Roe's Garden. "Dad gave mom the credit. Other people including people from dad's job weren't left out either. "Our yard was the neighborhood vegetable market minus the income we'd could have made, if pop's was business minded. "Hard work, no pay! "Besides the garden in the yard. "There we'd housed, The Mighty King! That was our dog. He'd prove to be the dog of dogs, that I'd matchup against any dog. "His doghouse maybe about a four feet from the alley. "A king is what he was". Foolish were the people that brought their dogs around to fight him". "Resume of King: His mother was a real wolf! "Father a full breed German Shepard! "A friend of dad's, that worked on the farm where King was born gave dad's friend a puppy. He in a kind gesture gave the puppy to our family. That was nice on his part, because dad was all the time looking out for him. "These people that owned that farm, would go to no end to help under privilege families, especially at thanksgiving, and Christmas. "A time to give back was an article quoted by the owner. "No family should starve! "Numerous finances we have. "We are blessed too giveback this charity gifts to them that are not as privilege as what we can do for others. "After hearing that bogus speech you'd think that he'd be campaigning for governor. One of his most noble displays of gift giving, was boasting about giving back to the community. "Every year it would be the same display of love for needy families. Though King was given to us, he wasn't a charity offering. king's profile: was dark as the midnight! "Black alpha male dog, was he. "Whose coat gleamed with the sunlight when the sun beamed down on his body. King had a dog chain that covered about most of the yard. "You weren't going to cut through our yard to avoid taking the block around Wayne Street to get to Market Street. The only way that would happen if King recognized your scent. Nobody ever got bitten by him for trying to sneak through the yard. "Lucky that! "I wouldn't want to see a pair of beady white eyes staring me in the face. "Then the following look of big sharp teeth. Getting ready to let you know, that your about to be dinner. "Then! "It happened! "Another time the kids from the West Gay Street neighborhood, came screaming through the alley on theirs bikes teasing him like they all the time did. "It was a tease where somebody was about to get too close to King. "This time while riding through the alley on their bikes; they'd thought less about the dog's position in the yard. "Stupid kids, King's chain was loose this day. "Coming through screaming insulting words, picking at the dog as if it were another day to tease the dog. "However the surprise was on them. "King's chain wasn't firmly attached to the ground. "King jetted out like a torpedo being launched from control-station. "Now the kids got scared. "Here comes this big black dog that looks like a wolf. "The kids are pedaling for their lives. "Like running from this escaped wild animal. "In all that ruckus these kids were pedaling, not too get away from my dog, but for lives as well. "Too get away from King; the big bad wolf. "Here he comes! "Most of them had made it. "Just the last guy wasn't so lucky. "King would lunge forward and catch a piece of the cyclist backside. "Yeah"! He was bit on his butt". "A nice piece of butt sandwich. "Umm!" I'm sure that's what King would've said, if he could talk. "We'll call the young fellow G-MAN. The prey that he was rewarded. First and only human victim of King. "He didn't make it through the course. A few, maybe four stitches was G-MAN's prize for being the slow one out of the bunch. The boy told his dad that he'd been bit by a dog that belonged to the James Family. After an exchange of words with G-MAN's dad, dad said that he'd pay the boy's hospital bill this time. "Told him not to look for anymore

Growing up in Westchester

handouts. Dad stated to G-MAN's dad that there wouldn't be a next time. "Any one of his kids or the pack which he hangs with, that they'd better have their own hospital money ready to pay their own bill. "They'd never know if King's chain was firmly fixed into the ground. Dad would mean that, because he'd seen his dog in action, beat the crap out of some poor dog. Besides, dad was getting tired of these wannabe dog fighter's, dogs coming across town to take an ass beat down from the King. "King showed the family something that was totally unusual for a dog. We'd have a chicken coop, that housed rabbits, ducks too. "Duck eggs came from that coop, and were some of the nastiest tasting eggs I'd ever tried. "Over my earth years, "I'd say I'll at lease try it before I'd forbid, myself from eating them eggs. "Duck eggs are out of my diet period! "Not an acquired taste! "Certainly off my menu. "Here comes a question! "What killed the ducks, the rabbits, and chickens? That was the question! "The next day would come! "Suddenly we're looking into a chicken-coop with no chickens, no rabbits, and no ducks. "They're all dead! "All but one! "How did it manage to elude death? Devine intervention is what took place. We'd name the surviving duck, Quack-Quack. "She'd have one duck foot, and a partial foot. Could she'd lost that foot while fleeing away from danger? "Call it an unsolved mystery! "And it didn't hinder her movement either. The A&P Food Market was a block away from my house. "Quack-Quack must've had this six sense about produce. "Believe this are not. She'd hobble her one-legged and half self through the alley, go across Wayne Street, straight up the alley to the A&P Food Store. "Then she'd start to eat off what green veggies were on the ground. It'd got to be such a ritual with her and the A&P produce truck driver, that he'd leave a pile just for her. Then after her share of eating, she'd hobble back down the alley, cross Wayne Street, came back to the yard. "Get this! "She'd sleep in the same doghouse as King. "I'd call that, "Devine Intervention! "Wow! "What would you say that was? "Like he was her protector. "Strange as hell wouldn't you say, that was? "Until some heartless motorist bastard, saw it as a sport, no doubt, well what choice of words, would you use to describe that asshole, for striking down an innocent harmless creature as Quack-Quack. "You decide for yourself." Prick! "Verdict's in! "That bastard saw to it, that, he'd would cancel any further trips through the alley, for the duck, no more crossing over Wayne Street. "She'd take her final trip to the A&P. "Never again would the produce trucker have to leave a side dish for her. "Don't look for her! "She'll not return to her eating spot. Never, never! "Thank that devil, that ended her moment of joy. "So long Quack-Quack. "You've made it home, for good! "Wayne Street and Market Street would've this curse that whenever it came down to an accident occurring, it happens on Wayne Street, and Market Street. "The accident street. "I'd come to call it. "The same rout I'd always take to the house. Through the alley three houses down, I'm home! Wayne Street is notorious for its busy traffic, would've me frustrated as I waited for the traffic too let up. "I'd must've waited over five minutes, "while trying to cross over to my side of the street". "Then when I'd thought it was safe, "I'd scurried across the street". "I'd would have made it, "except the last car behind me", he did bump me. "The driver of the vehicle came running to me as if he was surprised that he'd hit me. "As he'd came closer to me, I'd just gathered myself, than took off running up the alley to my home. Some bystanders that witnessed what had happened came to the back of the yard; where dad must've been feeding King. "The man now looked nervous, somewhat scared, for he'd didn't know what to expect when confronting my dad. Ecstatic, the man started talking to dad. I don't know to this day if he'd gave dad some money. "Everything back when I was a little boy, young guy that I was, it would involve some shady dealings, or cover ups, me being bumped by that motorist was just another chance for that motorist to get out of a hospital bill. "No bones broken, give dad a few dollars, and Everyone's happy. "Another cover up! "Not once was I'd taken to the hospital. "I'd guess that dad thought, I'd didn't have to go. "So why waste any money on another hospital bill".

CHAPTER 4

"1799"! "Westchester did establish its first fire company. Though the names have changed; an annual celebration was still being conducted as planned out every summer. "It was part of their annual Firemen convention feist. I'd wish to re-emphasize that Wayne and Market Streets was a cursed intersection, "just crying out for trouble. It would take place during the annual fire company celebration. "Conducted ever summer's end. "Each year the fire companies would start from their prospective fire station. Than they'd rev up their engines, turning their sirens up, without hesitation. "Then race from their own precinct all the way over to a dead end street on West Market Street. "That dead end section was a cul-de-sac. "Than once all the vehicles had arrived on station, they'd start the celebration. I'd almost became an ambulance driver, while on active shore duty during the Gulf War, that is what my job would've been, as responding to the war effort, so I'd only imagine what that power felt like, to be behind the wheel of an ambulance. "Furthermore as the party started to down sided towards the end of the day. The fire trucks would takeoff zooming back to its perspective station. "Now here comes the curse. "It'd be on Wayne and Market Streets. A Fire truck would hit a vehicle at the intersection of Wayne and Market Street. "The fire truck struck the side that the driver was driving. "Crushed, mangled that car. "This old model vehicle, saved that poor man's life. "Had it not been for the durability, the strong structure of that model vehicle, than this story I'd wouldn't be telling you this tale about, how the mangled car survivor, survived! "That man inside the car he'd would've died, but he'd escaped a certain death. "On impact, and I'd witness the crash, right at the moment it happened. "A welding team was called on to remove the driver from the car. "Torched that vehicle!", they'd have to remove sections at certain intervals too free him. "Jesus was with him. "It wasn't his time to go. "That tank of a vehicle would allow the rescue team to get the man out alive. "Mostly he was saved by the All Mighty. "For all you atheist nonbelievers, there is a higher power too! "He'd sent an angel in his time of need, that angel shielded him from a sure death. "Don't know how much money that man received from that tragic encounter, "Furthermore, he'd got paid! "The next day I'm back in my tree, that's at the end of the yard; picking Mulberries too satisfy my hunger. "That tree was the snack tree! " We'd have it, because nobody never had any money to spend at the corner store. "Thanks to God in Heaven for them berries. "Snack time, eat the mulberries"! Another thing, I'd might add about that Mulberry tree was the amount of pounding from the hammers we'd used on that poor tree. Took a thrashing, it did, plenty of abuse from us kids". A basketball backboard was put up in that tree. An attempt to place a floor layer was pounded into the limbs. "We'd call ourselves trying to make a tree house. "Pounding on that poor tree. "That's the extent we'd go to create fun. "Not too let boredom manage our summer affairs is the mischief, we'd concocted, in our yard, but we'd stayed out of trouble. "The law never did come too our house, looking for any of my friends. Nor me as well. "Did you see, "The Lord of the Rings? "The Tree that talked in the movie! "It came to life! "If that happened while we were pounding on that old tree, senselessly putting nails in its bark, him just waking up, would've been a Casper the friendly Ghost moment. "It coming to life, gets the first scare! I'd probably would've done a number in my pants, or who knows what! "The tree nymph, as he's called made it quite clear about the torturing his fellow trees as they received demolition from the villians of third earth. "Yes it would have scared the dickens out of us. "First thing he'd say is put that darn hammer down. "It probably would've changed my skin color. "We were just doing what children do. "Try to have fun. However did that old tree handle that type of punishment, God only knows, it did. "I'm glad I'm not a tree. "Throw in the clubhouse; now you'd thrown together the latest version of the Little Rascals. "Hiking! That's another thing to do when boredom settles in at home. We put together small lunches, mostly balcony and ketchup sandwiches. "Ready set go! "A hiking we'd go all the way to Brandy Wine Creek. "This would be a cool family get together, minus dad. "Somebody had to work. "For the effort of staying up a bit late too gather all them night crawlers, it did payoff. "The morning of our fishing venture: "we'd have plenty of bait, and did end up throwing the excess into the creek. "The fish ate well regardless of the time we'd put out at the creek, it showed because we were bring home a prize catch. "We'd set out to make this a proud day to go fishing. "That we'd did! "Catching them wasn't know problem at all. "These fishes didn't know how to stop biting! "Didn't expect a fish bonanza day, that too is what it was. "Turned out to be a fun day after all. "A bonanza it was. "Will most likely give the majority of this catch too some neighborhood folks. "It's a neighborhood thing! "Looking out! "That's how we'd do it! "Take as many fish that you can clean! "Being poor had its moments, it brought together a neighborhood that watched your families back! "As a child, you'd wasn't getting away with doing something that you'd shouldn't have done. "The neighborhood kept the young ones in line. As for the fish this day the whole block ate fish: the menu would read; cat fish, blue fish, sunnies, bass etc., the effort for staying up an overtime to collect worms, would pay off; that's a goodtime; my time at the creek, they're biting so freely! Plenty tonight, I'll be sharing, come see! Look at my catch, "They're really biting. This fish won't send me home empty handed, want to come home, and see our catch! "We'll be eating with fish on the menu. "With me! "Wow, I'm impressed! "We caught a load this time, the fish like me, and I'll just keep catching them. "We're pulling them in, it seemed like every time, we'd cast our reels out in the creek. "Cat fish, "come and get um they'll all be on the dinner table tonight! "We'd caught plenty of fish this day. "Nothing to frown about. "The fish are hungry, invigorating at best. "We'd have our share, so the rest can take this bait, and get bigger fishes for tomorrow, I'll be back! "Nobody gives away free meals all the time, be smart fish, take it and flee. The bait is a free dinner for the fish. "Actually we'd like you to grow fish, because the next time, I'm coming back to get you! "Good eating is what we're doing, I'm getting full, have some more, no thanks old friend, I've had plenty. "Mom make shore you fix a plate for dad's lunch! "With our own vegetables, from our own garden. "Sounds good! "Yummy! "Only terrible moment, at the time of the eating was cleaning them catfish. "They're still good, once the skin is removed. "Toss them in the fryer! "Come and get your order of fried fish! "An amateur I'd was. "After all that cleaning of catfish, it would take lots of practice too become good at cleaning them. Lots of practice! "Nah" I'll just leave it to the pro's. "However the scavenger fish that it is, "I'll still eat them up. "It's an acquired taste, that I'd learn to like. "And that's just good eating!

CHAPTER 5

"Did I'd get distracted from finishing the tour of the rest of the house. Well maybe I'd did! "Let's continue. We'd just came out of the kitchen. Standing in front of the stairs. We'll go up the steps. Mom, dad's room will be our next stop. "Here's a brief summary of their room: two windows in the front part of the room. Their bed was positioned between the front windows, and steps. They'd have room for their dressers on the wall in front of their bed. A closet on the same wall as the dressers, following the closet is the third window. Don't let me forget not to say the hole in the ceiling from the stove downstairs. "Needed heat rising up to all the above occupants room upstairs. "Last is the window in the back of their room. "From that window, you could climb onto the kitchen roof. "Mom, excuse me for saying this", you were an ungrateful child! You was handed a silver spoon. But you just wanted to waste your life with the loser of your time. "Instead, now you'd wish you'd have paid attention in school, and had went too nursing school. "your dream that you'd have talked about too your children. "No you'd settled for a child molesting womanizer. "I'd all the time did wonder, why couldn't I'd been an orphan? One they was given an opportunity like you was given? "Poor supervision on the part of my aunt. "You! "Your mom placed you in the hands of a person that was surely capable of providing you with a better lifestyle. "Surely capable than your own mother could've giving you. "But your aunt failed you! "So sad! "Put in charge! "But you'd didn't take charge auntie! "She'd bring many things from her childhood days, her inseparable toys, she'd bought with her into this house. "Now we have a readymade family to contend with, but it was more a case of a baby trying to raise babies. "It didn't work, because, my eldest sister was placed into a reformatory school, until she'd became twenty-one. "One toy was her Chatty-Cathy-Doll. "Remembering it well, when you'd pull the string, it would talk to you. "Poor doll, she was tortured by us boy children, constantly, continuously. We'd must've pulled that string, until one day it said, I'm through! It stopped talking, for good! "That's the end of the talking doll baby. "Now there is our room. "A junkyard by comparison, at least, because it was packed with our clothes, toys, and other miscellaneous debris, all packed in our bedroom. "Not the best room of the house, but it has to be mentioned. "Our existence too society, is the final contribution that makes up this family clan. "Frankly, I'd should've been born. "At the entrance to our room, a door was place there too close off access into our parents room. We'd have to knock before entering into they're room. "Now when going up to our room, there'd be a ledge on one side of the wall. "This ledge would allow us children to walk out on it. We could reach across and touch the wall on the other side of the steps. It was dangerous, but fun. "You'd have to have good balance and coordination. "If you fall off, some serious damage might happened to you. "Like maybe a severe leg or arm sprain. "Might even be broken. "All the more reason that dad told us that he'd better not catch us out there on that ledge. "Children never worry about the troubles that might harm them, until the accident happens. "Well then, it's always too late. "I'd was a daredevil child. Not too much of anything could discourage me from a challenge, mostly a challenge that would allow me to steal the spotlight for just long enough to get the girls attention. "I'd learn by showing off, it did get me some play from the girls. "I'd always pick the wrong girl. "The one that was a prostitute. "The one that seemed too revolve like a door. "That was my introduction into falling in love, and getting my feelings crushed. "I'd learn see them fast girls for what they were as my feelings kept on getting hurt. "The emotional excitement, helped me change from the guy that kept getting played, into the guy that became a player. "True what goes around does comeback. "This time you'll be running the show. "Bring on the excitement! "That's my slogan! "I'm going to play that tune. "I'm down for it! "This will be my moment of triumph. "I'd try to beat them at their in game. "At least once, I'll hurt you, momma, at least once. I'm going to impress the girls. "Back when I was young teen, I'd lacked the nerve to go up and talk to the girls. "So I'd try to impress them by doing something foolish. "Lucky, that I was, "I'd never broke any bones. "A few sprains that healed over time. "Dad could see the adventurous side in me, however, he'd expected me to lookout for my younger sibling brothers. "That I'd did too the best of my ability. "Brothers, Frank, Ric, even Kev knew that the ledge was off limits to them. Dad would stress that fact over, and over to lookout for them. "That's what he'd meant! "So that's what I did! " Off to the third floor! "Hot! "August, humid as all hell could unleash on us children of the third floor. "Fans were the best thing we'd have to use too try to stay cool. "Say what! "Are you kidding, trying to tell a joke or something. "What would save us some nights was a nice breeze from the trees. "Being up on the third floor, had its moments. "Accept when it was humid! "You'd pray for a strong wind too come into the room, a good breeze, when it did happen would cool the room off, like standing in a freezer! Like alka seltzer, oh what a relief it was too have that breeze. "The good thing was when it was really humid, we'd stay out front all night until the humidity, started to die down, then it would cool off the room. "At last cooler conditions would enable us to enter the room. Us children constantly suffered up there on the extremely hot third floor. "Watching them old gladiator movies, "heat stress had had to be a normal occurring event for them Roman slaves. "Are room did feel just like that. "Being stuck inside that that room was the equivalent of being stuck inside one of them Roman Dungeon's. "In the room we'd have a Queen size bed; that all eight of us children shared for a while. One of the elite eight, I'll call them that to protect the innocent, they'd wet the bed. "I'm just not going too exposed the child's name! "The bed wetting caused me to have uncontrolled sleeping habits. "Tossing, turning, getting up sleeping on the floor. "Times I'd hit the floor while maneuvering my body for only a second of comfort. "I'd should've offered my skill set to The Flying Wallendas! "Through numerous practice, I'd manage to sleep on the edge of the bed. "After a while, I'd learned to get comfortable, until dad would come into the room. "His signature wakeup sound, then the grabbing of the covers being removed. "You'd know than that sleep time was over. "At that time, I'm just starting to get comfortable. "That's when it would happen! "Like a drill instructor, after he'd removed the covers; that fatherly bark out of his voice, the command; "getup out of that bed! "It's funny when I'd recalled them moments, "an instance flashbacks of my boot camp, I'd start to relive them moments all over again." Why I'd have two boot camp experiences too add too my resume, it reads: "A Marine Corps Soldier, Navy Sailor. "The military had me go through boot camps. "Twice, and thank God I'm a survivor of both! "That's another story. "It, I'm talking about was going through basic training again worth all that suffering. "This time Navy boot camp! "Constantly worrying about the family I'd left back home. "I'm an insomniac, that's certain. "No getting around it. "I'm a person that has a hard time falling to sleep. "Want to know something else, that's why I'm writing this story. "Can't sleep! "Yet the Veteran's Administration just keeps giving me medicine that doesn't help. "I'd figure to get the right attention by stating this fact. "Why is it that a veteran goes to the VA for treatment of a problem incurred while in the service, and instead of getting medication to help them with their problem, the medication just causes them to become depend on the medicine, but it doesn't get rid of the problem! "I'm seeking a second opinion from a Dermatologist concerning why three/forth of my body is covered with a rash that keeps spreading. "Funny thing too is that the Dermatologist that I'm seriously waiting to get there second opinion from them. I feel they're about to cause me too have a nervous breakdown. "Why cause it's the same story I'd here when an appointment is being scheduled. "Hurry up and wait your turn. "Sorry! "Got off the topic about dad waking us up for school. "Today, he's coming in the room shouting. "He'd shout! "Getup for school now! After serving in the service, I'd often wondered about some of the strange acting borderline creepy folks that I'd met in the service, if they're dad treated them like being in boot camp, every time, it became time too getup. However can't cry to dad, and say that I'm still tired, cause then he'd might've snatched you up for just lying there trying to catch that extra wink. "I'd always hated the person who'd fall asleep on a whim. "I was never that person. Remembering all these sleepless nights. Singing out loud! "That's one of the few beatings I'd get from dad! "Making up songs when I'd should've been asleep. "I just couldn't fall asleep in a room filled with my siblings in the same bed. "So I'd take my punishment from dad for singing when I'd should've been trying to fall asleep. "But I'm still awake! "I'd missed my calling! "A natural songwriter is what I'd should've concentrated on becoming. "Receiving the fewest of beatings from dad, singing while I'd should've been resting was my family crime. "

No doubt, I should've been a songwriter. "That was my calling. " I missed my calling, I should've been a song writer. "A natural entertainer that I was! "Again who's going to take the weight? "With no financial support to harness my talent. "Everyone of dad's children had a special gift. "Ron invented The Inline Skates when he was in the first grade! "Mechanical skills, he'd have, "he was a natural. "We'd get these toy battery powered car models; and he'd end up putting mine together. "Again mad skills for a child! "Mozart was a prodigy, "Ron was a natural mechanic, just dad couldn't see his talent. "No financial support!

CHAPTER 6

"Batter's up! "Not, baseball! " I'm about to tell you about an intruder! "A flying black critter would come a calling into the bedroom. "Sister Donna was picking her toes on the bed, when this uninvited guest appeared through the ceiling. "Whoa family!", who gave it the right away? "Figuring he'd made his home in the wall was all the permission it would need to enter or leave the room through the ceiling. "No permit! "I'm A bat! "The speed of my wings is all the admission price posted with my flight. "Here it comes into the room! "Quick reflexes were now about to take center stage. "Unveiled reaction, speed by fear of; "oh shit it's a bat! "They'd showed me quickness. "Everybody but me would make it down the stairs. "What I'd do? "Grab the sheet and pull it over my head as if it would matter. They'd came back in the room with dad after the bat had manage to find his exit out through the same hole that bought it in the room. "Out of the room it went! "Gone for the moment. "Once more Dad would enter in the room, give me that look, than his reply; stop acting like a big sissy. "His lecture would follow, "you can't keep hiding every time something frightens you. "He said, I have a daughter so no more running, I don't care if it's a bat, rat, nor any other creature. "Just like I'd put them boxing gloves on you, you'd better stand your ground. "He'd made that loud, and clear! "The James Crew would now be on a Mission Impossible. "Get rid of the bat! "What we'd do next was too assemble all the children in mom's room. "What about ammunition? "Crazy, oh no guns just a broom, small shovel. "I'd guess that'd be enough firepower. "We'd have a broom"! Are you for real, as real and armed as we'll get! "Silly me! "Immediately I'd thought about the Wizard of Oz. We're going to take care of the wicked witch. "No not a witch this round, just a bat, an uninvited guest! "Up to our bedroom we'd go. Donna has the broom; then she'd start hacking at the hole in the ceiling. She'd must've disturbed it. "Looking at the hole, here it comes! This time I'm not last. I'd be leading the retreat. First one out the room! "Down the steps I'd go, making it to the last step, then I fell. "I'd slipped on the last step. And to top things off, here comes the family stumbling down on top of me. The shortest boy in the family, I'd blame my height reduction, lack of height due to them coming down, and falling on top of me. "Ha, ha, my joke! Back upstairs. We'd have to get that bat out of our house. In the room, at the hole in the ceiling another crack at it. The bat must go! "Again, Donna starts to poke inside the hole. Out comes the critter. A good swing by Donna this time, and she'd hit the bat, into the wall, it slammed against it with a loud crash, like them captions on the Batman and Robin television Series. "Wounded now, Rick smashed the bat for good. "The bat now lays wounded on the floor. "Ric would get a jar! "An old mayonnaise jar, then he'd stated that he's going to take that bat to school for show and tell. "Sharing one bed, eight children was pure hell. Eventually! Cheney State College gave us a bunk bed, two sets of dressers, with a twin bed added to the deal. "Believe me that was a true blessing. "Still all of us children would share that room. "But having a Bunk bed provided some breathing space, though we boys still had too double up on the bunk beds. "A well deserve gift that was. "It gave freedom to the boys for sure, thus allowing the bed wetting culprit to sleep in their own mess. "Making progress on the house tour, you'll travel with me back downstairs". Let's go into the basement. "My description would be:

one window, and a cluttered basement. Anything else that we'd could find too place in storage for added insulation got stuffed in the basement along the walls, where junk insulation was stacked up where it was mostly needed. "Good thing there wasn't a stove down there. "We'd have made a breaking news story; flash a family's house went up in flame in Westchester, no survivors! "Live on every news channel. "Cluttered was okay for the winter time. Spring time, start your cleanup! You'll need to start organizing things in the basement. Don't need to make any headlines about spring cleanup. "I'd just had to take some initiative. "For sure, take charge! "Youngman, "so try and be careful. "No accident please! "All the James family needs is an accident too take place. "Why the family is accident prone! "Fires or what not, be careful! "I'd didn't mind helping with the organizing of the cellar cleanup. "That helped build my character. "Plus we'd needed to move things around, while cleaning up the cellar. "Once more I'd be showing some initiative on my behalf. " I'd learn to start taking on some responsibility. "Besides space will be needed for the pool table. Room, now we'll have extra places available to put items whatever needs stored away. "Room for the pool table we'd have. "No need to contort your body when taking your shot on the pool table. "Room for playing knock hockey is available as well, also added in place, now we'd have a couch with a few chairs. "We're ready to start entertaining! "So I'm in charge of putting the basement back in order. That didn't take a moving company to handle that job. The next day, just playing around on my pool table, I'd wouldn't have notice it, if I'd hadn't taken a double look. "Oh shit I'd screamed! I hate rats! "Even too this day! "Dad at once came scurrying down the steps! "Shouting what the hell's wrong with you boy? "That's when I'd pointed to that big rat that was rumbling through the junk over by the wall. "That rat had to be seeking shelter or something like that.

"But again he was an uninvited guest. "He'd have to go! "It was a huge sucker, that it was! "Dad being the tuff father that I'd known him to be, grabbed that extra mop handle minus the cloth, forced that poor critter into a corner, than commenced poking it until it was dead. "Dad was fearless! "Must've had lots of practice as a younger child. "Playing in the sewer as mom often spoke about the stories he'd entertained her with while he was courting her. "His wild tales, as a child strengthen him up for whatever came at him. "Like fatherhood! " Too him it would mean the world. "Too him, I'd understood that so much, for he was a child growing up without a father. "Not having a father figure in his life. "He'd have so much to prove. "And I'll say this about my dad, despite all the arguing and fighting that I'd witness between mom and dad, he'd never abandoned his children. "Now being that tuff father was something he'd embrace like an anvil. "The rat! "Nor any person or critter was going too harm his children. "True to his word, my dad backed his words up, even if it meant going to jail. "Now this rat Needed handling. "Furthermore after he'd saw to it that the rat couldn't do anybody harm, "Dead now, he'd picked it up by the tail, "than took it out to the trash can. "Once again he'd looked at me, then said stop acting like a sissy". I have one girl and that's enough. "Nothing else was said about the rat. Couldn't wait till Friday or Saturday. "Stay up late watch television until television starts to watch you. Dad most of the time was next door acting as house bouncer. "Dad stood five feet seven inches tall. He'd wouldn't take shit from nobody. "Dad had a reputation to back up his play. Most people did respect my pop. Many of mom's, and pop's arguments stemmed from him being at that lady's house next door. "Woman can have some of the strangest thoughts that they allow to go through their head, while being involved in a relationship. "Dad mostly went over there to let off steam. Get free drinks for assisting the old hag. "A hag is what that lady was, and where ever did mom got the notion that dad would have an affair with that wicked witch of the east, than mom should've seen a psychiatrist. "I'll second that play because even if she'd were the last woman on the planet, "I'd commit suicide. "Than to be caught in bed with a hag like her. "Some men have no morals, I guess! "But I'm certain for sure that dad wouldn't stoop that low! "Or would he? "They'd fought too many times after he'd leave her place. "Some fights, they'd wakeup the whole block! "As I'd stated earlier, I was stunned that our family stayed together. "Any day it could've been the next time that the police, the ambulances, child services, or an agency to displace children, would step in and take us too live elsewhere. "We'd survived that one. "God is Good, but somehow my parents forgot that! "The Hag's drunks kept coming out of her house I'm just was watching them through the window, many staggering, too make it out the gate. "It was a ritual like routine being played out every weekend. "Knowing what drunks do when they'd known that they'd have had too much to drink. "Looking for comedy than just watch the drunks, they'd be heavily intoxicated, tune in an see an old bar scene reenacted next door. It's better than watching television. "Plus it's free. "No charge! "Lots of them would come staggering out of her home. She'd made her money. "Surveillance was put on her place by an undercover barhop, she'd have no idea until the police undercover officer would give the police enough information to proceed with a raid. "Then one day it happened, her place got raided. She'd did run an illegal drinking spot. "They'd called them, Speak Easy Joints! "Dad was arrested! "Now mom would need help! A child on the way, and a husband caught up in raid! "No time to play around. "Who will pay the bills now that dad's been arrested? Keep your head up high mom! "She'll find a way! "Hard times, tuff lady she was all mom! "And that she'd do. She'd got her man released from that raid, at the next door neighbor's house. "Dad got out, no doubt, she'd got them to release dad from the raid on the Speak Easy. "I'd felt her cousin being on the force did help her cause. "Still the strong black lady that mom was, however, she'd didn't use that wisdom to provide a better life for her children. "Mom was all that and some more. "But just didn't see the light at the end of the tunnel. "I still love you mom! "Amen! "It was on a Saturday morning when my buddy's parents were taking his family to Hershey Park. "An Amusement Park located in Hershey, Pennsylvania. His parents had offered to take Ron, and I with them. In the we're hours of the morning, Ron, and I are getting ready till something drew my attention to the yard next door. Zeroing in on that big oak tree. Investigating the situation further, "Oh my god", a woman was tied to the huge Oak tree in the yard. "She was being whipped like a runaway slave, "after being returned to its owner. Unfortunately, I'd recognized who the woman was. "Coming out of the bathroom. I'd waste no time telling mom what I'd witness. "Mom wasn't impressed not one bit", just said, hurry up and come out of the bathroom! "Finish getting dressed in the front room, "she'd say! "Nothing mattered to mom, and pop! "Mom would tell me later on that, that was a husband and wife problem, that dad said to stay out of it. "But still! "He'd had no right to whip that woman like that period!" "Nothing else was ever mentioned about that subject. Sadly! She was a beautiful lady, but because of her promiscuous behavior it would be her downfall. "Stabbed to death by one of her lover's. A horrendous stabbing it was. I'd think it was the same guy that stabbed her a few times, from a previous encounter, they'd have in their home. "It's happening again! "Another episode starting up with her and her man. "Once more, she'd come" hurrying up the alley, her house was nearest to Wayne Street. Just a short walk to ours. "In a mobile home is where she'd resided. "It'd be easy for her to come up to our home, because no one else in her radius, would do anything for her. "She'd came to our house bleeding badly. Mom helped her by dressing up her cuts. "She'd wouldn't go to the hospital. "As if that mattered! "The only time that the cops or ambulance came in our neighborhood; it'd better had been to pick up a corpse. "Black Hispanic. let them kill themselves. "We'll supply the booze, the guns, and the body bags. "Then will just send in the cleanup squad. "A sad story, but it was my reality, back then, when I was young child! "Miss S than would get a change of clothes from mom, that belonged to my sister. " Peg wouldn't mind giving up them clothes from her wardrobe. She'd always have nice clothes. "As a grownup now, I'd came to understand why dad all the time would give Peg more money than the boys. "Girls deserve the most beautiful things period! "Peg was always getting a new outfit" She'd put on Peg's clothes, "would thank her, and mom for they're kindness. " She'd leave, and that would be the last time that any of us saw her alive. The gentleman that whipped her, while she was tied to the Oak tree was her husband, at that time, but like most marriages that go bad, add theirs to the list. They'd separated. "They're not living together as husband and wife. "He wasn't charged with any homicide activity the night that her body was discovered. "Farewell Miss S.

CHAPTER 7

"Dad had a few foolish friends. Two off them liked to brag about who was the better soldier. "They'd both participated in the Korean War. "On this particular night, at the house drinking with dad. They'd started boasting again. The two of them would take it this time to another level. "Grabbing what! "No they'd didn't! "Yes the fools did! "Each would go and get a pistol. Each from they're souvenir gun collection. "A prize display that both ex-soldiers contributed too they're spoils of war, now added to their war display case. "They'd both go out the house, than start reliving they're active duties, particularly the patrol scenes in pursuit of the enemy. "They're acting out combat moments of an enemy assaults. "Strong case for Post Traumatic Stress Disorder(PTSD). "Now! "Out the house they'd go to play war games. "Oh snap! "They'd actually went outside to see who would get caught first". That's precisely, what these two fools did. "Dad made everyone stay inside the house, for fear that one of us might get shot. "Curiosity killed the cat. "Yes I'd have to find away too investigate. "Like one of my favorite cartoon's; Johnny Quest. "Get down to the action, this is classic combat activity being performed right from my house. "And they'd taken it to the streets. "Bottom line, is somebody going to get hurt? "That's the question I'd want to know. "Two grown men setting a poor example for my family and me. "Why don't dad step up and tell them to take that nonsense someplace else. "Again dad's two foolish friends and alcohol stole the show right away from him. "I'd acted as if I'd had to use the bathroom. "Someone was in the yard. "I'd looked out the window, then did see one of the foolish partaker in the game. I'd distracted him by calling his name. "Good thing I'd did that, because that was all the distraction the other guy needed. "A chance to jump out from where he was hiding, and say drop it or your dead! "Swosh! "For a minute there I'd thought there was going to be a shooting. "Through all that melodrama, the two simpleton's wouldn't let the boasting stop about, who'd was the better soldier. "Like the boy said to the rabbit, silly rabbit, tricks are for kids. "One shot, a man could've been a goner, the other behind bars because he'd held on to Post Tramatic Stress Disorder(PTSD),and they'd didn't get any help from the Veteran's Administration. "Rumor had it that the youngest of dad's soldier friend got into a commotion at the Police Station. "They'd later found him hung dead in his cell. "Mystery again! "They'd never looked into his death. As far as my knowledge it could it had been another police cover up? "Believe it or not! "Now let's talk about man's best friend!

CHAPTER 8

"Have you ever had a special dog? Like, Lassie, Rin Tin Tin; The Pit Bull that was a police dog. "The one that took a bullet for Tom Hanks". "Oh snap, I'd remember that movie, because it made me cry when Hooch took the bullet. "A classic favorite Turner and Hooch. "Memorable Dogs! We'd had a few or more. Our yard I'd called it an unsanctioned dog kennel. "King whose doghouse was at the bottom of the yard. When we'd moved into a much bigger home, that still wouldn't have mattered, because his dog chain covered most of the yard. "Eastside of town is where will be moving. "Too start a new chapter into is a three bedroom house that wasn't any better than the house we left, except for the three bedrooms. "The basement was equipped with a furnace just that the basement now need more work done too it. Again, we're passed on to another hellhole! "The cellar although it did have a furnace, the floor was muddy, the basement needed to be dig out and fixed up making it look like a decent cellar. "There is the heating problem right out the gate. "Dad now I'm getting it through my head, loud and clear dad; don't be like me be better! "Don't throw away opportunity! "Don't let your fathers mistakes turn your life into a drunk, like him. "Making this new dump, will now be a challenge to start living in its new surroundings. "A second time, in another house, can't call it a new home, because there's an urgent need to start fixing the place up. "Once more, this is supposed to be a place where mom would be proud to raise a family, but it was just becoming like the last place. "A sinkhole of added headaches, "felt more like we're fighting too stay out of quicksand! "Still no section eight, nor home improvement is too come to this house either. "Getting away from this town was the shining light necessary to help keeping my chance for a prosperous future, not a life in and out of jail. "Chester County Farms as it was called when I was still in school. "Now it's the Chester County Prison. "That's where I was heading! "My criteria would read like so: high school dropout, Chronic marijuana smoker, loved too drink, worked as a janitor for Henderson High School. "That's the short version. "Dad's drinking would increase after losing his best job working for the Highway Department Of Transportation. At lease finally after all them so jobs, he'd have one with decent pay. "This job, dad might've had enabled him to put extra money aside for some home improvements. "Declined, and so did his dreams of any home improvement makeovers. "Lots of work to be done. "Now whose going to take the weight? "Has to be done by some one! "No way is dad going to make it happen. "He'd lost the best job too date. "Times running out for him! "Everybody is getting older. "Should've tried God like his brother did. "Shouldn't have to look so far down the road, but I'm not going to stop dreaming, because he'd let the bottle beat him. "I'm looking far down the road. "It's not going to be the next development. "No improve living conditions there wouldn't be none. "This is what must be handle possibly as living there would become our home. "Selection time for the doggies! "King would come along with us. "For sure! Surely it shouldn't had happen! " King's story is one with a sad ending! A family member was going to the store, located on the other side of Market Street. Market Street was and still is a very busy street in Westchester. "This incident was due from negligence on they're part. "He should've been on a lease. "I'd totally blame the family member for his death. 1;new area to the dog. 2, should've had him on a lease. 3; you'd set him up to get killed by calling out to him from the other side of the street, and expecting him to sprint through the Community Center field, unscaved , than have him jet across the street through the traffic. 5; that's where he'd met his fate. A motorist struck King down. "Hit him! "Drugged him under their car. "Then kept going after he'd done the damage to my dog. "King would summon together what strength he'd have left in him. "He'd staggered like a beaten fighter to his corner. "The curb was his final curtain call. "It felt like watching King Kong fall to his death. "The two Duchesses! The first one was an old German Shepard that kept getting pregnant. None of her pups would live after she'd have them. She must've of had about three liters of puppies. Once after all the disappointments, one finally lived. We'd named her Queenie. She became dad's personnel watchdog. If any of dad's friends came around, than started ruff housing with dad, Queenie would start to growl. She'd almost bit one of his friends. They'd no not to come in the house, than bother with dad while he was trying to rest in his favorite lounge chair. "Queenie's immune system would give way! She was lying in her favorite location next to dad's chair. He'd found her, then would bury her. "Mom said dad had tears in his eyes. "Too dad, she was the stray dog that he'd bought home. "Only to have to get rid of it. Duchess's number two dog. "She'd found her way back to the house. "Now number two Duchess just secure her spot in the James family circle. "That's what she'd did! "What! "No way! ""Yes way! "We'd be moving over to the east end of Westchester. "Dad decided that one of the dog's wasn't coming with us. He'd made the choice! It was Duchess the Boxer, who was coming with us. "A beautiful well breed mongrel was she. "Hair texture, was sandy brown, with a white underbelly. "Paws a mixture of sandy brown with white added in place. "A pure champion bred well dog was she; that She was indeed. "That same gentleman that gave us King gave us Duchess too. "Now he's a man, who highly believes in giving too the less fortunate. "Now he'll be traveling abroad. "It would be a business trip of some sort that will keep him away for quite some time. "Duchess was used to being around children, as the owner stated, so dad said, why not take her off his hands. "A family dog that loved children. "She'd taken a liking to our family the minute she was introduce to us. "Dad's connection came through one more time; first King, now he gave us Duchess, but for how long would we keep her? "After hearing that the choice to give her up, "it's not the right choice as we'd found out after dad took Duchess out to the country. "There he'd released her out of the car, than he came back home minus her. "Dad had made his choice, once again. "This thought kept echoing in my head, the one about pick, and choose. "Dad always made bad choices, giving up a chance at a better career, when he'd hitchhike from the Midwest too Pennsylvania. "Getting rid of the wrong dog, and she'd prove that by finding her way back to the house. "Dad had this connection of nice people, some I'd learned to pay attention too. "Others, I'd see them for who they were. "Leeches pulling him down, "they'd nowhere to come too get a free drink of liquor. "They wasn't your Friends dad, just a place to come sponge off of you, and your stash. "A strong trait that he'd possessed, a nice man who'd love to have the spotlight. "A gregarious man! "That's my dad. "liked the center stage. "He take a few drinks, That's when he'll start to perform, couldn't save that talent for the real stage, so he'd prefer the bottle as his audience, too assist him in what would be his slow death. "Cirrhosis of the Liver, plus cancer with other complications is how the coroner report would read. "It'd upset me immensely, when the First Sargent had called me in his office to present the news to me. "After hearing the news, I'd thought about going awol. "But I'll talk about that story in my next book. "Crying in the bottle, my dad, and his so called associates, not friends! "Backstabbers they were! "The majority of dad's associates were somehow connected to the foolish arguments, between mom and dad. "I'd believe that's what they'd wanted to see, knowing that a fight at some point would follow. "Giving reason for some person too run back too mom's aunt. "They'd loved too spread gossip too mom's aunt because off her status. "Well established her aunt was. "So that's what the hippocrates in our neighborhood sought out too do. "Too unexperienced young adult, with no way of knowing, that the cards were stacked against them. "Mom, dad, you wasn't getting a prize for embarrassing yourselves in front of the whole neighborhood. "All that was on the line, for your acting so foolish, was a reputation for becoming a woman beater. "So please stop the drama. "Dad never wanted to see the truth, but, I believe that he'd saw something in his future that must've frightened him, and it frighten him bad enough too want to give up a chance at success. "How dare you tell me too not be like you. "You was a quitter! "I'd agreed with that comment, the one where he'd say, don't be like me, be better. "The truth, now as I see it, it's not going to chase me away, I know with the Almighty, I can't lose! "So bring its own fear, stares me my face if you like, I'm going for the top! "Then the new house came up. "What to do next, about the dog? "The SPCA no, because you'd have to keep the dog fed while it is impounded there. Without an owner, she'd get euthanized. She was too pretty an animal to have an ending like that. Dad decided to take Duchess far out in the country, and leave her there. "It wasn't even a full week, that had gone by yet. "Surprised! "Everybody in the family was amazed to see her return. "No it was happiness! "Even dad too. "When he'd seen what she'd done on her own. "Right at that moment, she'd became dad's main dog. "Duchess took Fuzzy's spot and that choice didn't sit well with Donna. "Replacing Fuzzy, "no way was Donna going to let that transpire. Are family problem was that we'd all liked dogs. "Giving them away never came easy. "Fuzzy was an all white eskimo dog that was given to my sister Donna from the sister of Famed Movie Star; Eva Marie Saint. "No bull! "Her sister was married to a doctor who'd have his own office in Westchester. "He was a Medical Doctor. Donna at that time worked as a cleaning person for the wife. Fuzzy would mean so much to Donna. My sister had heavy thoughts of suicide. "Somehow though Donna was able to find Fuzzy a home. "She wasn't living with her, but now she'd have visiting rights, on a day to day basis. "Donna was the most luckiest of all the family members. "How you'd might ask? "She'd had a nose for finding money. "My family was a family of adventurers. "We'd be walking through alleys, far out of the way of our neighborhood. "Donna would get the notion to look in a trash dumpster. She'd fine money. She'd always lookout for the family. "I'd believe that's why she was so blessed. "God rest her soul. "Once, "She'd found over a hundred dollars in the dumpster. "She'd gave mom more than half of it. That was the type of sister, that Donna was. "A strong giving heart. "Westchester used to have a train line that ran through the town making many stops to Philadelphia. The tracks where the train ran on, above the tracks, next street over was The Gay Street Bridge. They've removed the bridge, and now it's a flat road. "But before that had happened. "Back in the day, Donna loved to come flying across that bridge. "Like the top of that bridge was her launch pad, as in a Ski Jump, she'd hit the top of the bridge at full speed, than soar almost to the corner. "Not quite but close enough! "No shit! "She was hard on shocks absorbers. "That was fun watching her do that, we the younger boys just went along for the excitement. Than they'd smoothed out the road, made it look

Growing up in Westchester

strange for that street. "That bridge would've had plenty of stories to tell if it had a voice. "Donna was the original Wonder Woman so she'd thought. "A broken arm bought her back to reality. "Then later on she'd thought she was one of The Dukes of Hazards. She'd loved to hit that bridge at full speed. By the time we'd reached the top, we'd be flying like Speed Racer in the Mach five. "She'd land maybe twenty yards are less from the corner of Adam's Street. As a young boy that was so cool, too watch. "Not having Fuzzy living at home with her would let her know that it was about her time to move on. "She'd meet this man, he was older than my mom and pop. "Raised Donna's two daughters, like they were his own. "Across the alley from where we now reside. "Four twenty six East Miner Street. "Our new residence! "There's this empty old abandon garage that we'd adopted it as our new playing area. "This would also be the burial spot for Duchess, the Boxer. "She'd went missing for a couple of days. "It wasn't like her to just disappear. "Duchess, is discovered by a neighbor. "A friend to the family, who was playing in the garage. "Resting peacefully for all times is Duchess the boxer. "The dog that we'd given a full name too. "And she'd responded to every name we'd call her by. "Her name was Duchess, Ralph, Arc, Gone Dog! "Why she'd have them names? Duchess is royalty. She was a royal boxer! Ralph! "She'd have the arrogant of the Scottish Bull Dog without the pipe. I'd imagined her looking like Mac Gruff the crime dog. "Pipe in her mouth, and the British Fog Cap. "Arc the way she'd arch her back awaiting for someone to call her. "All the time wiggling her nub of tail. "Oh how she'd slobber. "Dog mucus running down her face. We'd say; growling the words out gone dog. "Then she'd thought she was getting punished. "We'd send her away! "Then we'd show affection, when calling her back, once more. "Always wiggling that nub tail. "Dog hands down is man's best friend. "Our family had enough dogs to substantiate that claim. We'd learn that the eastside of Westchester was burden by many kids who turned out to be trouble makers. "Also were a bunch of nasty miserable minded old people, or might I say sometimes cruel folks, that didn't like animals. "Duchess fell victim to somebody's cruel prank. "Missing, poisoned, left to fend for herself. She'd didn't have the strength to find her way back home again. "The family all salutes you. "Duchess Ralph Arc Gone Dog and she was prematurely taken from us. "By my belief, my readers, "we'd have been better off staying on the west end. "A family member kept getting into trouble. "He found it easy to steal without getting caught. "The stealing may have seemed like fun, just like all good things they have to come to an end. "Again getting involved with the wrong crowd of people. "And it did come back to haunt him. "Certain for sure jail time will either wake you up, or compel you too keep getting sent there. "Not me! "I like my freedom. "Being a criminal wasn't the way I wanted to go. "Crime I'll pass on that one. "Lost Duchess to mayhem! "This was certain! "That the James Family kept a memorable dog. "For us, losing Duchess would now give us the dog I'd call the basketball dog. "Every time, a new dog would enter our family, that dog would have its own story to tell. "Thus creating their memorable moments. "Enter Ringo the basketball dog. "Say the magic words, and he'd come running after the ball. "The attention getter was to start bouncing the ball. "Now say the attack word! "Which is; "Hud-hudda! You'd better have good handles own your basketball when dribbling it. If Ringo got his teeth into it, you'd be buying a new ball. "I'd lost a few". Ringo was definitely a memorable dog. "Hud-hudda! "So long my friend! "You'd made it possible for me to have Curly Neal like handle of a basketball while dribbling it. Curly Neal without question was the Greatest basketball dribbler, that I'd ever witness, in his performance as a

Harlem Globe Trotter. "I loved playing basketball, but it wasn't my calling. "Who was Curly Neal? "One of the Greatest Harlem Globetrotters whatever laced up a pair of sneakers. "Assignment! "Check him out for yourself in Basketball Digest, enough said, about him. "Hear Wolf! "He'd come to me recognizing my special Trill high-pitched vocal sound, in my voice, when I'd call him. I'd used that trill, it was his way to know that it was me. "Sure each family member was recognized by their own way of calling him. "But our acknowledgement too each other was special. You'd really have to get to know Wolf. "Like King, you just couldn't enter the yard. "He'd bark first, then start to growl if you'd wasn't recognized by knowing or calling out too him, so that he could acknowledge your voice, then", You'd better not come in the yard. "Four years I'd been away from Wolf. "Now I'm in the military. Stationed on the west coast at Marine Corps Base Camp Pendleton, California. "First duty station. "Assignment, Correction Battalion. "No I'm not a prisoner there. I'm a new staff member. "All Marine! "My next book is about how I'd dealt with two different branches, and did find success at both. "Tune in for the next book, entitled, wait, I'll tell you about it next book. "First duty station has opened my mind too what it's like to be on your own. Four years, I'd spend on the west coast. "My time now is about to come to its end as a Marine. "Homesick for the east coast, I'd get out after my enlistment had ended. "Let's do something you'd haven't done before. "We'll take the bus back to the east coast. "Seeing parts of the United States has, bitten into me like a Rattle Snake. "I'm going to travel if, I'm ever given that chance. "Why travel abroad? "There's plenty to see right here in the Good Old USA. "Proud to be an American. "Can't wait for the next time too travel. "Give me some tickets. "Ready set let's go see the USA. "Traveling to places, I could now identify and talk about them. "If I'd seen them on the "Travel Channel. I can speak something about that place. "that's so cool! "Nothing better than too be able to share your experiences thru state or world travel. "I'd do my four years, than return back to the east coast by Greyhound Bus. Realizing now that, I'm doing what dad told me not to do. "My shot was using the Marine Corps as a learning platform to educate myself about the ways of the world. "Being on the west coast did that for me, but I'd allow doubt in myself, just like dad did, than turning away from the opportunities that the Marine Corps presented to me. "Foolishness does run in my family. "Scared to take the plunge! I'd ran home! "Not too mom, just I'd try something different. "Chief Warrant Officer James didn't sound too bad. Now that I think of that label. "Experience taught me, don't cry over spilled milk, clean it up, than get yourself some more! "Instead I'd get homesick. "Somehow after all that focus to get back into school, get your diploma, go into the service, somehow I'd lost that edge! "Cherishing my accomplishments is what I'd should've been doing. "Back home I'd go. "Up to the house about to try the backdoor to see if it were unlocked, like it all the time was. A dog's bark, then a growl would proceed the bark ."I'd call out to Wolf! "Voice recognition was confirmed by Wolf! "Barking seized! "Now he's wagging his tail. "He'd acknowledged that his master was back home. Responding with our only way of communicating! "The here Wolf with the trill added. He's Happy to hear my voice. "Funny thing, if he was able to talk, he'd would've said: where the hell you've been man?